DISCARD

America, My Country
American Heroes

Lewis and Clark

By Doraine Bennett

Clarke C. Scott, M.A.
Content Consultant

STATE STANDARDS PUBLISHING LLC

Your State • Your Standards • Your Grade Level

Dear Educators, Librarians and Parents . . .

Thank you for choosing books from State Standards Publishing! This book supports state Departments of Educations' standards for elementary level social studies and has been measured by the ATOS Readability Formula for Books (Accelerated Reader), the Lexile Framework for Reading, and the Fountas & Pinnell Benchmark Assessment System for Guided Reading. Photographs and/or illustrations, captions, and other design elements have been included to provide supportive visual messaging to enhance text comprehension. Glossary and Word Index sections introduce key new words and help young readers develop skills in locating and combining information. "Think With Bagster" questions provide teachers and parents with tools for additional learning activities and critical thinking development. We wish you all success in using this book to meet your student or child's learning needs.

Jill Ward, President

Publisher

State Standards Publishing, LLC
1788 Quail Hollow
Hamilton, GA 31811
USA
1.866.740.3056
www.statestandardspublishing.com

Library of Congress Control Number: 2011931737

ISBN-13: 978-1-935884-40-8 (hardcover)
ISBN-13: 978-1-935884-49-1 (paperback)

Printed in the United States of America, North Mankato, Minnesota, August 2011, 060611.

1 2 3 4 5 - CG - 15 14 13 12 11

About the Author

Doraine Bennett has a degree in professional writing from Columbus State University in Columbus, Georgia, and has been writing and teaching writing for over twenty years. She is a published author of numerous books for children, as well as magazine articles for both children and adults. She is the editor of the National Infantry Association's *Infantry Bugler* magazine. Doraine enjoys reading and flower gardening. She lives in Georgia with her husband, Cliff.

About the Content Consultant

Clarke C. Scott holds degrees from Central Michigan University and has 31 years of experience as a classroom teacher, building principal and system-wide administrator. Clarke currently serves as Director of Middle School Education and Lead Director for History with Pittsylvania County Schools in Virginia. He enjoys hiking, kayaking, caving, and exploring Virginia's and our nation's history. He shares his adventures both above and underground with his wife, Joyce, and three grown children.

Table of Contents

Hi, I'm Bagster!
Let's learn about
American Heroes.

Meriwether Lewis was born in Virginia.

Time Line

1774
Lewis is born

Meriwether Lewis

Meriwether Lewis was born in Virginia. He lived near Thomas Jefferson. Jefferson was a leader in Virginia. Lewis knew Jefferson. Lewis was in the army. He served in the West. He liked nature. He wrote about plants he saw.

William Clark was born in Virginia, too.

Time Line

1770
Clark is born

1774
Lewis is born

William Clark

William Clark was born in Virginia. His family moved to Kentucky. Clark liked being in the woods. He was in the army, too. He served with Lewis. The two men were friends.

Lewis was the president's helper.

Time Line

1770
Clark is born

1774
Lewis is born

The President's Helper

Thomas Jefferson became **president**. He led the country. He asked Lewis to be his helper. Lewis said yes. Lewis wrote letters for Jefferson. He told Jefferson about the army. They talked about the West. Jefferson trusted Lewis.

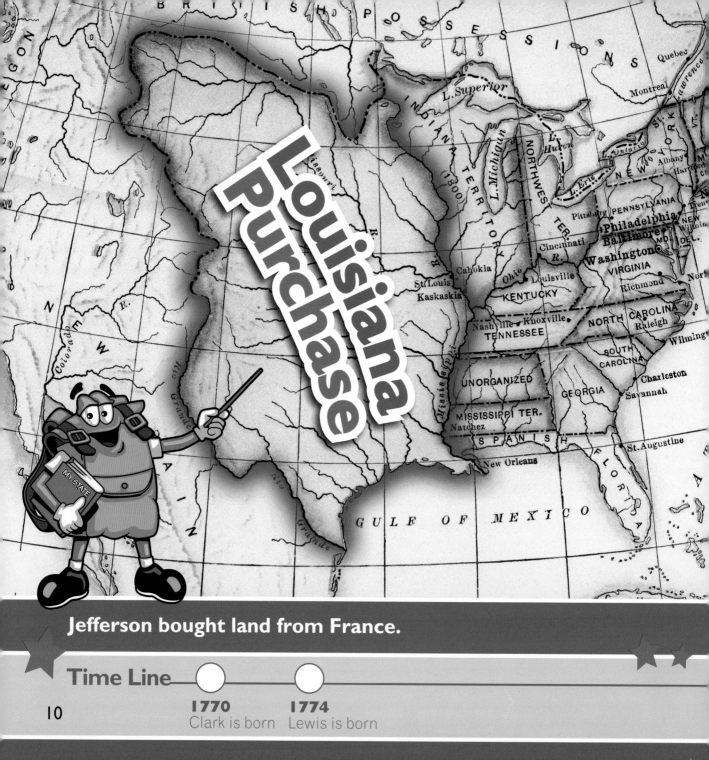

Louisiana Purchase

Jefferson bought land from France.

Time Line

1770
Clark is born

1774
Lewis is born

The New Land

Jefferson wanted America to grow. France owned land that he wanted. He bought the land. It was called the **Louisiana Purchase**. Jefferson wanted to know all about the land. Did the rivers flow to the Pacific Ocean? What animals lived there? What plants grew there? Were the Indians friendly? Would they trade with the Americans?

Lewis and Clark set off in boats.

The Trip Begins

Jefferson asked Lewis to go and see the land. Lewis chose Clark to help him. They picked men to go with them. They needed strong, young men. It would be a long, hard trip. They set off in boats. The trip was filled with danger. Clark had a **slave** named York. Clark owned York. One day Clark fell into a river. York saved Clark.

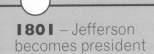
1801 – Jefferson
becomes president

1803 – Buys
land from France

1804
Trip begins

13

They told about waterfalls and snowstorms.

Time Line

1770
Clark is born

1774
Lewis is born

What They Saw

Lewis and Clark kept records. They told about the dangers. About fast rivers. About waterfalls. About mountains they climbed. About cold nights and snowstorms, rattlesnakes and bears. About huge animals called **bison**. They hunted for food or traded with Indians. They made maps of the land.

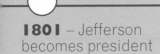

Sacagawea helped Lewis and Clark talk to the Indians.

Time Line

16

1770
Clark is born

1774
Lewis is born

A New Friend Helps

They tried to talk to the Indians. But they needed help. Sacagawea and her husband joined them. Her husband was a **trapper**. He caught animals. He sold their furs. Sacagawea was an Indian. She had a baby. She helped Lewis and Clark. She did not guide them. But she did remember places she had been before. She helped them talk to the Indians.

Say Sacagawea: *sah-kah-guh-WEE-uh*

Lewis and Clark reached the Pacific Ocean.

Time Line

1770
Clark is born

1774
Lewis is born

It's the Pacific Ocean!

At last they reached the Pacific Ocean. They were filled with joy! The waves were huge. They looked like small mountains. Lewis and Clark searched the **shoreline**. They searched the beach. They found a dead whale on the beach.

Lewis and Clark's maps helped people go west.

Time Line

20

○ **1770**
Clark is born

○ **1774**
Lewis is born

Going Home

It was time to go home. Indians helped them on their way. The trip lasted over two years. Jefferson welcomed them back. Trappers and **traders** went west. Traders buy and sell things. Lewis and Clark's maps helped them. More and more people wanted to see the western land. The country grew. Just like Jefferson hoped it would.

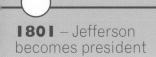
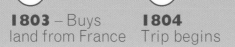

Glossary

bison – A huge animal that lives in the West.

Louisiana Purchase – Land in America that Thomas Jefferson bought from France.

president – A person who leads the country.

shoreline – The place at a beach where the land and water meet.

slave – A person who is owned by another person. Slaves are made to work against their will.

traders – People who buy and sell things, or give things to people in exchange for what they want.

trapper – A person who traps wild animals and sells their furs.

Word Index

Editorial Credits

Designer: Michael Sellner, Corporate Graphics, North Mankato, Minnesota
Consultant/Marketing Design: Alison Hagler, Basset and Becker Advertising, Columbus, Georgia

Image Credits — *All images © copyright contributor below unless otherwise specified.*

Think With Bagster

1. Why did Thomas Jefferson ask Lewis to lead the trip? Why did Clark go on the trip? Would the trip have been different if Lewis had lived in Massachusetts or Georgia? How?

2. What did Lewis and Clark hope to learn on their trip? What did they really find?

3. Name some people who helped Lewis and Clark. How did they help?

4. How did Lewis and Clark's trip help America grow?